EXPLORING THE SUN

Messner Books by William Jaber

Exploring the Sun
Whatever Happened to the Dinosaurs?

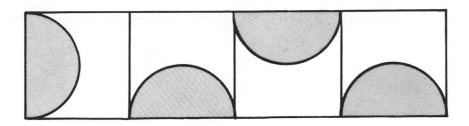

Exploring the Sun

by William Jaber

illustrated with drawings and
photographs by the author

JULIAN MESSNER ⬤ NEW YORK

JULIAN MESSNER and colophon are trademarks of Simon
& Schuster, registered in the U.S. Patent and Trade-
mark Office.

Manufactured in the United States of America

Design by William Hogarth

Library of Congress Cataloging in Publication Data

Jaber, William.
  Exploring the sun.

  Includes index.
  SUMMARY: An introduction to the sun, its features
and movements, how we use its energy, and legends
concerning it.
  1. Sun—Juvenile literature. [1. Sun] Title.
QB521.5.J32   523.7   80-10985
ISBN 0-671-32997-9

Acknowledgments

My personal thanks go to several organizations for their cooperation in answering all my queries, filling orders for photos and other information. Chief among these are California Institute of Technology, some of whose photos help to explain the text.

I am also indebted to the Lick Observatory, University of California, and to Dr. Donald J. Williams and the Space Environment Laboratory for their generosity in filling my orders for information and photos. To Science Service, Incorporated, I owe a note of thanks, for it was their small weekly, *Science News* that has kept me abreast of happenings in solar astronomy. I might add that none of these should be held responsible for any shortcomings of the book—these would be mine.

I am especially grateful to my editor, Madelyn K. Anderson for her continuous encouragement and helpful criticism, and to Lee M. Hoffman for feeding me many news clippings and advice.

Finally, I want to extend my thanks to my sister Jo Ann M. Jaber for her valiant efforts, hard work and infinite patience. She typed the manuscript and offered a great deal of constructive criticism.

And, as always, my wife Dorothy suffered through the inconveniences and interruptions to daily life which a project of this sort always seems to generate. My thanks to her.

William Jaber

To the memory of
Jean Joseph Robinson (1924–1978)
my friend and colleague. His
talent and integrity have been
and will always be my inspiration.

Contents

 # Warning

Do not ever look at the sun directly through any telescope, or any other glass or lens device. This is an almost certain way to be blinded for life. The sun's rays are concentrated by lenses or glass, and this concentrates the harmful kinds of wave energy that beam down along with the sunlight.

And be aware of added danger: a blinding injury can be suffered without realizing it until it is too late. It takes less than one second for a permanent injury to occur when looking through a telescope directly at the sun.

The makers of telescopes give warnings, but these do not seem to be sufficient. Every year eye injuries do result from this cause.

Always use filters or smoked glass to view the sun, and always get advice on these from experts. For example, many telescopes are fitted with caps designed to protect the eyes while watching the sun. But these often snap suddenly from the concentrated heat that falls on the telescope. Such an accident may result in a blinding injury if the viewer fails to react soon enough to the bare lens with the searing solar image on it. Play it safe, view the sun *indirectly* by allowing the telescope image to hit a suitable background surface. Experiment with types of surface to get the best images.

Don't use binoculars to look at the sun under any circumstances.

Introduction

It's almost 10 A.M., Sunday, February 25, 1979. The sky over the prairie of western Canada is clear. The air is crisp and very cold. The sun is shining brightly, its rays glinting and sparkling off the clean, fresh snow.

In the little village, people are shoveling snow from their walkways. One of them is ten-year-old Shaun Mankota, the son of the owner of the village inn. The Mankotas are Cree Indians, and the walk Shaun is shoveling is in front of the largest building in the village. It is a three-story green and white house, with a large neon sign on the roof that reads "Oak Tree Inn." Oak Tree Inn is owned and operated by the Mankota family as a hotel and restaurant. They also live in one part of the building.

Right now, the inn is nearly full of guests. One large group has just arrived.

Shaun has stopped shoveling and is standing in the yard, thinking about these latest guests—13 men and 10 women. He was annoyed that they had laughed at the name of his village: Sundown.

Shaun looks for his father, who is repairing a light switch in the kitchen. "Papa, who are these people who just came? And why do they laugh so much at our village's name? And what's. . . ."

"Whoa, now," interrupts Mr. Mankota. "Not so fast. One question at a time. They are astronomers from the University of Minnesota. They are scientists who study the stars—that's what astronomers are. And they are here for a special reason. Tomorrow, here in Sundown, will be the best place in all of Canada and the United States to see a total eclipse of the sun. Do you know what an eclipse is?"

Shaun thinks for a moment and then answers half-heartedly, "I think I know, Papa. My science teacher told the class Friday that there would be an eclipse here. But I forgot what she said about it. I know it had something to do with the sun and the moon. Is that why they were laughing at our village's name?"

"Well, sort of, son. But you should have listened and paid better attention to what your teacher said. An eclipse, as I understand it, is when the moon moves across the face of the sun. It blocks out most of the sunlight. The sky gets dark and the stars come out. Chickens are fooled into thinking that it's evening, and they begin to look for a place to roost for the night. Bats and owls are fooled, too. They think it's night, so they come out of hiding and hunt.

"But in only about five or six minutes, the moon moves off and away from the sun. The whole world gets brighter and brighter, just like in the morning—only much faster. Even the bats and owls get caught in the daylight and have to scamper back to their homes. All this will happen right here tomorrow."

"But I don't understand, Papa. Why can't the astronomers look at the sun through a telescope any time?"

"Well, when the moon shadows the sun's face, the scientists can see parts of the sun's surface that are

14

usually hidden by the glare at any other time."

"What do you see when you look at the sun through a telescope, Papa?"

"Well, sometimes you can see giant flames shooting up off the sun's surface, and dark spots, and other things."

"The sun must be very hot and very big. Right, Papa?"

"Yes. One scientist told me that the sun is so big it could hold a million earths and still not be full."

"That's scary," says Shaun. "Suppose the sun

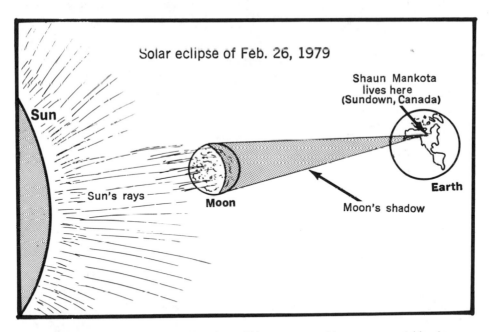

Solar eclipse of Feb. 26, 1979

Sun

Shaun Mankota
lives here
(Sundown, Canada)

Earth

Sun's rays   Moon   Moon's shadow

This is how the sun, moon, and earth would have appeared to someone watching in outer space on February 26, 1979—except that the sun is much larger and much farther away than the drawing can show. The sun's rays go out in all directions. When they strike the moon they are reflected back. This causes a shadow on the side of the moon away from the sun. That shadow is cast on the earth's surface when the moon moves between the earth and the sun.

15

gets too close to us, or one of those flames gets too big? That would burn us up, wouldn't it?"

"It certainly would," answers Mr. Mankota. "But that's not likely to happen. The sun is very steady. It has been shining like it is now for millions of years. And

the chances are very good that it will continue to shine just like that for millions of years more.

"And I don't have any more time to talk, Shaun. Maybe our visitors will tell you more. But don't make a pest of yourself.

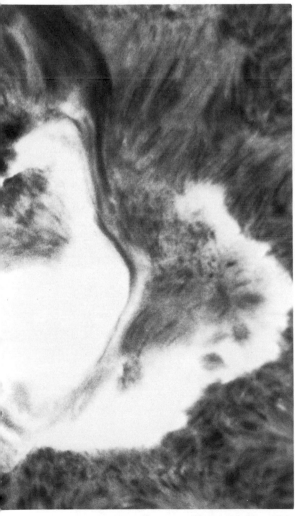

A gigantic solar flare, photographed through a telescope using a special red light that cuts down the glare. This photo brings out the stormy appearance of the sun's surface during the time it was being photographed.

Courtesy Hale Observatories

17

"These are very nice people, Shaun, and if you help them whenever you can, maybe tomorrow they will let you look through one of their telescopes.

The next day, the day of the total eclipse, Shaun helps many of the scientists, in all the ways he can. And they return Shaun's favors. They not only let him look through a telescope, they let him look through several kinds of telescopes. He can see a giant flame through one telescope. The scientists say it is a "solar flare," and it is bigger than the whole earth—maybe even bigger than two earths. They let Shaun take a color picture of the flare with one of the cameras attached to the telescope.

Shaun tells his father, "Now I know why they were laughing at our village's name, Papa. They were not making fun of us. They came here to see two 'sundowns' in one day—both in the village of Sundown. We could not have a better name for the village. I'm very proud of that name, Papa."

Shaun decides right then to become an astronomer—a solar astronomer who explores the sun. It is an exciting adventure . . .

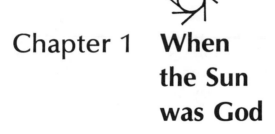

Chapter 1 When the Sun was God

People worshipped the sun in many parts of the world until about 2,500 years ago. The best known example of sun worship is to be found in the religion of ancient Egypt. The sun god of Egypt was sometimes associated with the wind and so was called Amon-Ra. But at other times he was associated with life forces and was given the name Aton-Ra. *Ra* means sun.

Throughout most of the history of ancient Egypt—a civilization that lasted more than 3,000 years— the sun was chief god among many gods. Egyptian kings, called pharaohs (fare-ohs), were regarded as sons of the sun.

Pharaoh Ikhnaton (ik-náh-ton), who ruled in the fourteenth century B.C., believed in only one god, and that god was—the sun. Ikhnaton forbade the worship of any god but the sun god Aton.

But his son-in-law Tutankhamen (too-tan-kah-men) destroyed Ikhnaton's religion of Aton. When Tutankhamen reigned as pharaoh, he restored the old religion, which worshipped many gods. However, he did leave the sun as chief god.

Before we say how "dumb" people used to be, remember that no one had a telescope to see the sun better. That instrument is less than 400 years old. And the camera, which is so important to the astronomer today, is only a little more than 100 years old. People could never have discovered any of the facts about the sun without a telescope and without the other complex machines that present-day astronomers use.

In the days before there was any science—up to about 2,500 years ago—most knowledge was based on what had been learned through people's senses: sight, hearing, smell, taste, and touch. Human beings knew the sun only through the senses of touch and sight. They felt the heat of the sun as its rays touched their skin. With their eyes, people saw the sun "rise" above the eastern *horizon* (the farthest point you can see). Then they saw the sun "move" across the sky and "set" or "sink" below the western horizon.

Their senses fooled them. What they saw was not the truth at all.

They saw the sun "rise" and "set," but it was not the sun that was moving—it was the earth. And the sun is really much larger and much farther away than it appeared to their eyes to be.

Like the Egyptians, many other ancient people thought the sun was alive. They thought it was a god who guided their fortunes, who gave life, and who brought destruction by changes in the weather.

Certain kings and religious leaders taught that the sun was alive and ruled the earth. This idea of a living, ruling sun god became part of the religion of millions of people.

In ancient China the sun was a minor god. He was sometimes chased about the heavens by a great, evil dragon. And sometimes the dragon caught the sun and began to bite big chunks out of it. The ancient Chinese treated this as a time of great crisis. They feared that the dragon would eat up the whole sun, and the world

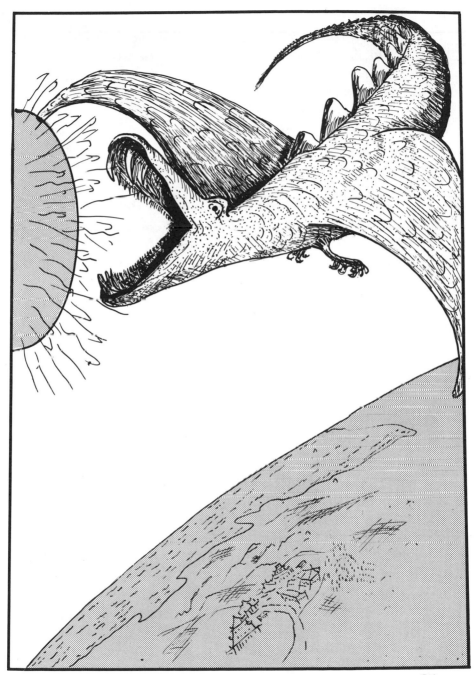

would be left in darkness. Without the sun, life would be doomed. So when they saw the dragon attack, the king would order his soldiers to shoot arrows into the sky, hoping to frighten away the dragon. It always worked, too. The dragon would "spit up" the sun, and slink away to try again some other time.

This is the ancient Chinese explanation for a solar eclipse like the one Shaun Makota saw in February 1979.

Other cultures had essentially the same reasons for believing in the sun as a god: when the sun was down—"gone"—the earth was dark and often very cold. It was night, a time of fear and mystery. The only lights people had then were torches and fires, or the light of the moon.

And because there was so much else in the world that was unknown, people just naturally believed in ghosts, monsters, evil spirits, and many other evil beings who came out mostly at night. Shooting stars, fiery comets, many kinds of strange natural lights, and the flights of night animals such as bats and owls—all these scared people. Night was a time of terror especially for travelers and for children. Even today many people are frightened by these things and of the night.

And besides the night, there was the fact that the sun moved toward the south every year, at about the same time. Its rays became weak, and as this happened the world grew cooler, then cold. The land was battered by fierce storms with high, cold winds, and the nights were deadlier than ever during this time of the year—the wintertime.

Many animals, such as insects, died. Others, such as bears, crawled into holes and slept all winter. Still others changed their colors or their coats of fur.

Birds flew south, following the sun and its friendly warmth. But people could not do these things.

And to top it all off, there was still another reason why winter was a fearful time: would the sun ever return? No one could be sure. If the sun did not return, the world would be in everlasting darkness and cold. Flowers would not bloom, plants would not grow. There would be no food. The animals and people would die.

Because of this terrible fear, ancient people set up a watch for the sun's return. On the mornings of December 21, 22, and 23, all eyes would be turned toward the southern sky. Up to now the sun had been moving further and further south every day. If the sun was going to return, it would begin to do so on one of these days in late December. It was always at this time in the past that the sun stopped moving south and began its return to the north. But they could not be certain that it was happening again until about the twenty-third or twenty-fourth day of that month.

When the skywatchers became certain—and it was never later than December 24 that they became certain—that the sun was returning, the glad news was shouted everywhere. A great feast was prepared, and people came out into the streets to dance and shout with joy. Big fires were lit and food was brought out—*Sol Invictus*, or the "Feast of the Unconquered Sun" began. The world was safe for another year.

The ancient Romans celebrated *Sol Invictus*, their greatest holiday, on December 25. The early Christians, Roman subjects, could not compete with this holiday. So they did the next best thing: they moved the celebration of the birth of Christ, which most scholars believe occurred in the spring, to December 25.

The celebration of *Sol Invictus* was weakened as

Christianity grew and sun worship slowly decreased. The discovery of new scientific facts about the sun solved some of its mystery, and this, too, helped to make sun worship less popular.

Although sun worship died out in Europe with the rise of Christianity, it lived on in the Americas for another 1,000 years, until the European conquest led to its disappearance in most cultures.

Chapter 2 The Founding of Solar Astronomy

The story of solar astronomy—the study of the sun as a star—began over 6,000 years ago, in a civilization that is older even than that of ancient Egypt. This civilization was founded in western Asia between the two great rivers Euphrates (yoo-fray-teez) and Tigris (T-eyé-grihs). Because it was located between two rivers, it was called Mesopotamia, which means "land between the rivers."

In ancient Mesopotamia, the sun was a minor god; the moon was the principal god. The first astronomers were priests who kept careful records of the motions of the sun, moon, and stars.

About 3,000 years ago, the records were so complete that astronomer-priests began to see that heavenly bodies often followed regular paths, or *orbits*, through the heavens. These orbits were so exact that the astronomers were able to predict where some heavenly bodies would be in the sky at any time of the year.

Mesopotamian records showed that the moon moved in a regular, predictable orbit around the earth. It completed one trip every 27 days, 7 hours, and 43 minutes. The moon's orbit was so well charted that it was used to divide the year into twelve nearly equal parts, called months. Each month was the time it took the moon to make one orbit of the earth. We adopted those divisions for our modern calendars.

The Mesopotamians also discovered that after 223 trips around the world the moon would move in front of the sun and its shadow would block all or most of the sun's light. This is called a *solar eclipse* and it occurs every 18 years and 11 days, a cycle called the *saros* by the Mesopotamians. They regarded *saros* as proof that the moon was better, or greater, than the sun—it could block out the sun's light.

This gave ancient astronomers their very first hint of both the distance and the size of the sun. These facts were to become the first discovered in the field of solar astronomy. The Mesopotamians reasoned it out this way:

If the moon can move in front of the sun, then the sun must be much farther away from the earth than the moon is. And, since the sun and moon appear to be about the same size, even though the sun is farther away, the sun must actually be larger than the moon, too.

Again, they reasoned: if two people stand face-to-face and begin to walk backward, each will think the other is getting smaller. That is because each sees the other from a greater distance.

Thus, solar astronomy was born. From that time on, our knowledge of the sun has steadily grown.

Now we have traced the story of solar astronomy from its earliest beginnings in the religions of ancient civilizations. Later scientists kept on asking questions—new questions. And they kept on finding out more and more about the sun. But when the age of science dawned, about 400 years ago, people still knew little more about the sun than was known 5,000 years before, in ancient Mesopotamia and Egypt. In fact, it was less than 200 years ago that the respected scientist William Herschel claimed that the sun had living things

In baseball, a player in the infield, say at third base, looks much taller and larger than a player out in the outfield. The ancient Mesopotamians reasoned that the sun looks smaller than it really is because it is much farther away than the moon.

on it, under a bank of fiery clouds.

We know for certain now that this is not true. The sun does not even have clouds. They could not exist in the great heat the sun produces, up to millions of degrees Fahrenheit. No one could live there nor even within a few million miles of its surface. The sun's heat is enough to melt anything on the earth—anything.

We have learned more in the past 50 years about the sun than had been learned in all 6,000 years of recorded history.

It is the task of science to discover the truth, and astronomers have searched for the truth longer than anyone else—astronomy is the oldest science in the world.

Chapter 3 **World of Giants**

Because the sun is the biggest single object we will ever see during our lifetime, exploring it just naturally takes us into the world of giants: giant objects and giant numbers.

Everything in astronomy is gigantic—even the telescopes. They are among the largest machines ever built.

The telescope was invented, in about 1608, by a Dutch lens maker named Jan Lippershey. Two years later, Galileo, a scientist in Italy, was the first to use the telescope to look at the heavens. From that day on, new facts about the heavenly bodies were added almost daily.

During the next few generations, using increasingly stronger telescopes, astronomers discovered three new planets—Neptune, Uranus, and Pluto—charted thousands of stars and hundreds of galaxies. They also learned how to measure distances between heavenly bodies.

And then came the camera—invented in France by Joseph Niepce and J. M. Daguerre, sometime between 1829 and 1838. This instrument caused another revolution in astronomy, because it is more accurate for seeing distant objects than is the human eye. Cameras were attached to telescopes and made permanent records in the form of pictures.

Suppose you lived 2,000 years ago, along with the Roman emperors, and were given $1 billion to spend but only at the rate of $25 a day. Would you have spent it all by 1980? The answer is no. You would have spent only about $18 million in those 2,000 years. And you would go on spending $25 a day throughout the rest of your life, your children's lives, and on and on for another 8,000 years before spending the last of your billion.

If someone were living in this galaxy and photographing us, this is how we would look. This galaxy and ours are called spiral galaxies because as they move, their arms spiral—like a Roman candle.

Courtesy Lick Observatory

And our sun, which is a star, is only one of 100 billion other stars in our galaxy, the Milky Way. And the Milky Way is only one of billions of other *galaxies*, or groups of stars.

By using complex cameras, telescopes, and other machines, and a lot of mathematics, astronomers have found out the size, temperature, and many other facts about the sun and other stars.

Astronomers know that, although our sun is huge, it is small im comparison to some others in the galaxy, called *giants*. In fact, our sun is a *dwarf* star—a yellow dwarf. Yellow stars are of medium heat and brightness. The hottest and brightest stars are blue, the coolest and dimmest are red stars. These colors can only be seen through giant telescopes or captured on film by telescopic cameras.

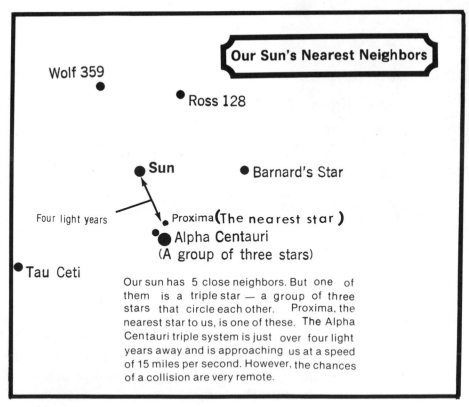

Our Sun's Nearest Neighbors

Wolf 359

Ross 128

Sun

Barnard's Star

Four light years

Proxima (The nearest star)

Alpha Centauri
(A group of three stars)

Tau Ceti

Our sun has 5 close neighbors. But one of them is a triple star — a group of three stars that circle each other. Proxima, the nearest star to us, is one of these. The Alpha Centauri triple system is just over four light years away and is approaching us at a speed of 15 miles per second. However, the chances of a collision are very remote.

This 200-inch telescope is one of the world's largest and most expensive machines. To get some idea of its size, look at the door and table in the center bottom of the picture.

Courtesy Hale Observatories

In the twentieth century, better cameras, many complex measuring and recording machines, and computers, began to be used by astronomers. With the new instruments, the first major question the astronomers attempted to answer was, how far—how far is it from the earth to its nearest star, the sun?

For over 2,000 years, most figures given for the distance between the earth and the sun were little more than guesses. Measurements of that distance today are

33

made using highly complex electronic methods, and these are checked by other often equally complex methods, such as those using *satellites* that orbit the earth. Besides using all these methods of finding the sun's distance from the earth, scientists still use telescopes for that purpose, too.

We cannot deal with all the various methods. But we can pick the most popular, and least complex, one and show how it is used to find the distance. But before doing so, it would be of value to know what that distance is: the sun is 92,000,000 miles (148,000,000 kilometers) away.

How far is that? Such figures have no meaning if we don't understand them or cannot imagine them.

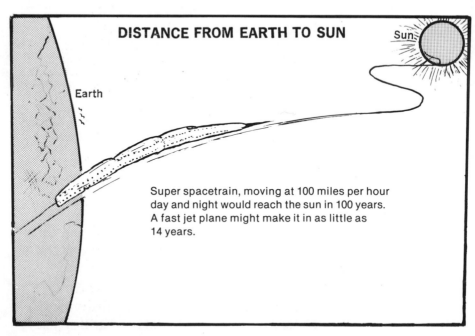

DISTANCE FROM EARTH TO SUN

Sun

Earth

Super spacetrain, moving at 100 miles per hour day and night would reach the sun in 100 years. A fast jet plane might make it in as little as 14 years.

One way to get a "feel" of the distance from here to the sun is to use a comparison. Imagine yourself traveling there by train. This great sky train leaves the earth, zooming through the clouds and up into outer space at a speed of 100 miles per hour. It travels at that same speed day and night—it never stops. How long would it take the train to reach the sun? It would take almost 100 years!

Or, let us go by another means of travel—a fast jet plane. It takes off, gets up to the speed of sound, at about 600 miles per hour, and like the train, holds that speed all the way to the sun. How long would it be? Well, if you were 15 years old when you left the earth, you would be 43 years old when you returned. It takes about 14 years each way at this speed.

However, there are other things that can travel much faster than any plane or train. These other things can go to the sun in just a little more than eight minutes! They are light and radio waves. Both travel at the speed of 186,000 miles per second. If an airplane could fly at the speed of light or of a radio wave, it could circle the earth at its equator seven and one-half times in just one second.

One way to measure the distance to the sun is by means of *radio waves*.

Most of us don't even know what a radio wave is. But don't be embarrassed—scientists don't know much about it, either. Mostly they tell us what a radio wave is by what it does. A radio wave is not something you can touch. It is a form of *energy*. And energy is the ability to do some kind of work—any kind of work. A radio wave is very similar to another kind of energy called *electricity*. But electricity, or electrical energy, is much stronger than radio waves. It can hurt you. Radio

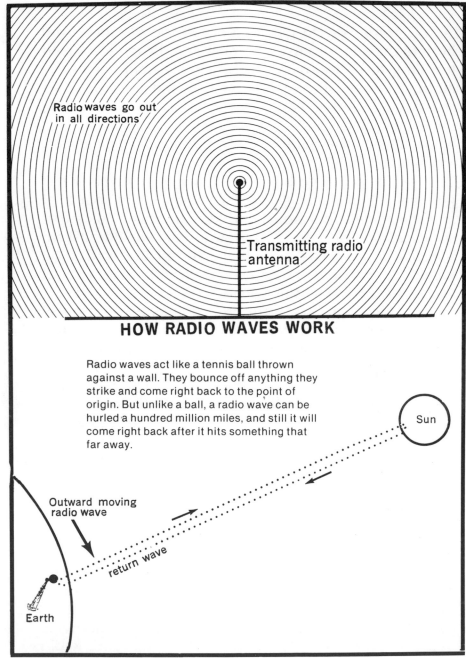

Radio waves go out
in all directions

Transmitting radio
antenna

HOW RADIO WAVES WORK

Radio waves act like a tennis ball thrown
against a wall. They bounce off anything they
strike and come right back to the point of
origin. But unlike a ball, a radio wave can be
hurled a hundred million miles, and still it will
come right back after it hits something that
far away.

Sun

Outward moving
radio wave

return wave

Earth

waves cannot hurt you; they go right through you and you don't feel them. You cannot tell where a radio wave is unless you have a special kind of machine that acts or moves or does something when a radio wave strikes it. The special kind of machine that can detect radio waves and catch them is called a *radio*. A "sender" or *transmitter* is a machine that is used to send out the waves.

If we cannot touch radio waves, it must be hard to tell what they look like. But scientists do know what radio waves look like, and you can, too. All you have to do is drop a pebble into a still pond of water. Tiny waves move outward and downward in the water from where you dropped the pebble. If you could see radio waves in space, this is what they would look like—except that radio waves move outward in all directions, while the water waves move only outward and downward. And, as we said before, radio waves travel at a known speed—the speed of light, which is 186,000 miles per second. This speed never varies—that is, it never increases or decreases.

A radio wave also bounces. It is the greatest bouncer or "rubber ball" you will ever meet. It acts like a tennis ball or handball hurled against a wall. The ball comes right back to you, at least some of the time. But a radio wave will come right back every time. Not only that: you can "throw" a radio wave 100 million miles using a transmitter, and if it strikes anything—zoom—it comes right back.

So all you need to know to measure the distance to any heavenly body is the speed of the wave and the time it takes for the wave to return after having been sent. It takes 16.5 minutes for a radio wave to go to the sun and back. That works out to 8.25 (eight and one-quarter) minutes each way.

There are 495 seconds in those 8.25 minutes. If you multiply the speed of the wave—186,000 miles per second—by 495, you get 92,070,000 miles (or about 148 million kilometers), the distance it traveled to reach the sun.

Of course, that distance varies a little because the earth does not travel around the sun in a perfect circle. We are closer to the sun in winter than in summer. That sounds wrong, because summer is warmer, and so it feels like we are closer. But the earth is tilted in such a way as to take the sun's rays more directly in summer than during the winter. When the sun is more directly overhead, as it is in summer, its rays are much stronger and carry more heat.

The size of the sun was first measured by complex mathematics based on three principles of planetary motion. These principles or laws were discovered by Johannes Kepler (1571–1630), a German astronomer. Astronomers have since used Kepler's laws to find out many other facts about the sun, such as how much it weighs and how thick, or dense, it is.

We can imagine the size of the sun if we again compare it with something. For example, the moon orbits the earth at·a distance of 240,000 miles. Now, if the earth were placed in the center of the sun, and the moon placed in its same orbit—240,000 miles away—the moon would still be 94,000 miles under the surface of the sun. In other words, the sun is much larger than the whole earth-moon system.

The sun is 865,000 miles across. It would take 72 earths, side by side, to stretch across the face of the sun.

The volume of the sun is how much it can hold. If a bottle holds a quart of milk, a quart is the volume of

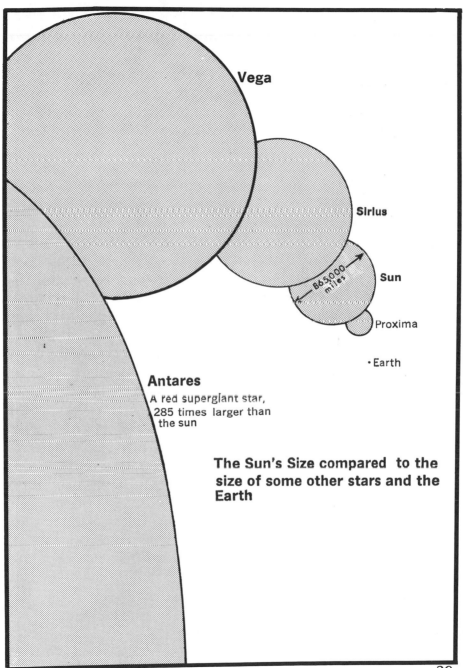

Vega

Sirius

865,000 miles

Sun

Proxima

· Earth

Antares
A red supergiant star,
285 times larger than
the sun

**The Sun's Size compared to the
size of some other stars and the
Earth**

the bottle. What is the volume of the sun? The sun can hold *one million earths*.

That means the sun has a million times the volume of the earth. Yet it weighs only 300,000 times more. Why does the sun weigh so little compared to its volume? It is because the sun is not a solid body. The sun is a huge ball of glowing gases.

If we could put the earth on a scale, its weight in tons would be the number 66 followed by 20 zeros, or 6,600,000,000,000,000,000,000 tons. And to get the sun's weight, you have to multiply that by 300,000!

The sun travels at about 150 miles a second around the center of the Milky Way. It makes one complete trip around the galaxy every 200 million years. The fact that it is moving at 150 miles per second and it takes 200 million years to circle the galaxy tells us a little about the size of the Milky Way.

To further understand the size of our galaxy, we have to pause and talk again about the speed of light. The speed of light is used for measuring distance in outer space. The distance light will travel in one year at the speed of 186,000 miles per second is called a *light year*. The light year is a kind of "yardstick" or means of measuring vast distances in outer space. There are 31 million seconds in a year, and so you have to multiply 186,000 times 31 million to get the number of miles light travels in one year. And the Milky Way galaxy is over 60,000 light years across. No wonder it takes the sun 200 million years to make one trip around the galaxy!

Again, it is plain to see that there are no numbers bigger than those used in astronomy.

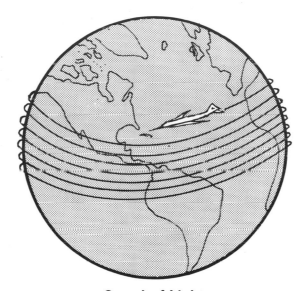

Speed of Light

An airplane flying at the speed of light could circle the earth seven and one-half times in just one second.

Chapter 4 The Sun's Motions

The sun does not move around the earth, as it seems to be doing. That is an optical illusion. An *optical illusion* is seeing something that is very different from the way it really is. It is different from a *mirage*, which is when you think you see something that is not there at all. Seeing a pool of water in a desert where there is no water at all is a mirage. But here is an example of an optical illusion:

You are sitting in a train looking out of a window. On the track next to your train is another train waiting to leave the station. Suddenly you see that you are moving past the other train. You pass by the windows and the cars of the other train, faster and faster, and finally you pass the last car of that train. And it is only then that you realize it is not *you* who is moving—it is the other train, pulling out of the station. This kind of illusion happens very often, and it's an interesting experience.

In the same way, it is the turning of the earth that makes the sun appear to be moving. But it is we who are moving—not the sun.

This illusion was not discovered until a few hundred years ago, but the ancient Greeks suspected that the earth was moving. They noted that the stars, moon, and planets moved, too. It occurred to the Greeks that it was much easier to imagine the earth turning

THE ROTATING SUN

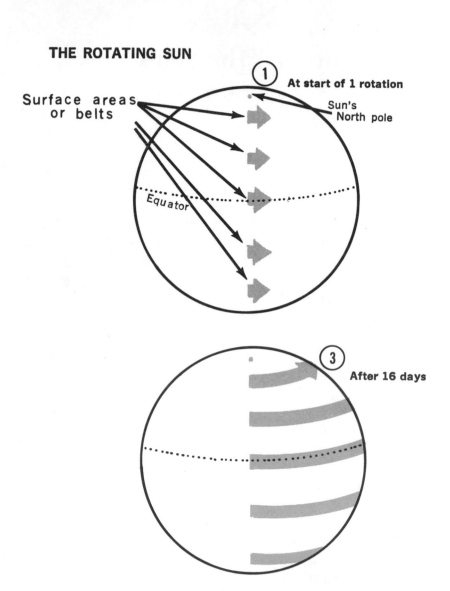

At start of 1 rotation

Surface areas or belts

Sun's North pole

Equator

After 16 days

Because the sun is made mostly of gases, its rotation is very different from that of the earth. The middle surface, near the solar equator, makes one complete rotation in about 25 days. But the regions or belts close to either pole go around once in from 26 to 30 days.

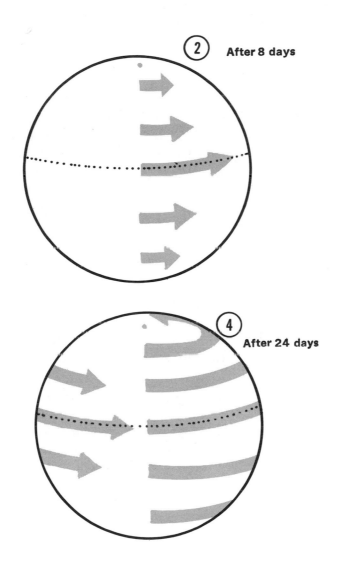

round and round (which is called *rotating*) than to imagine the whole universe turning, which is the way it looks. So they decided the earth must be turning.

And with the same reasoning, some ancient Greeks even reached the conclusion that the earth moved around the sun, making one complete trip each year. They were right, but their idea could not be proven, and so scholars decided to forget it. For the next 1,500 years most people believed that the sun revolved around the earth.

It was the Polish astronomer, Nicolaus Copernicus (1473–1543), who proved the ancient Greeks' belief that the earth revolves around the sun.

The sun has two motions: it rotates on its axis, and it moves on a longer journey through the galaxy, taking its family of nine planets—the solar system—with it.

But the sun's rotation is very different from that of the earth. For one thing, the center or equatorial surface goes around faster than the surface at either pole. That is because the sun is a gaseous body, not a solid.

The middle or equatorial region moves all the way around in about 25 days. The surface regions that lie about half way between the poles rotate more slowly— once every 26 days. And at the north and south poles of the sun, the surface makes one rotation in a little more than 30 days.

Spring - Summer

The sun

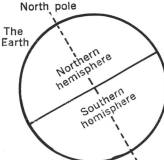

In spring and summer the earth's north pole is tilted toward the sun. This brings the sun to an overhead position for anyone living in the northern hemisphere. And the sun's rays strike the earth more directly, thus giving more heat.

Fall - Winter

The sun

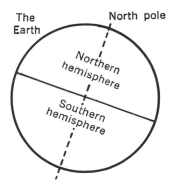

In fall and winter the earth tilts away from the sun, and to people in the northern hemisphere it looks as if the sun has moved south. And the sun's rays no longer strike the surface directly. So the earth's northern hemisphere gets less heat. This is what causes winter.

Chapter 5 Features
of the Sun

The temperature of the sun is over 5,000 degrees Fahrenheit at the surface, but it rises to perhaps more than 16 million degrees at the center. The sun is so much hotter than the earth that matter can exist only as a gas, except at the core. In the core of the sun, the pressures are so great against the gases that, despite the high temperature, there may be a small solid core there. However, no one really knows, since the center of the sun can never be directly observed.

Solar astronomers do know that the sun is divided into five layers or zones. Starting at the outside and going down into the sun, the zones are the *corona, chromosphere, photosphere, convection zone*, and finally the *core*. The first three zones are regarded as the sun's atmosphere. But since the sun has no solid surface, it is hard to tell where the atmosphere ends and the main body of the sun begins.

Corona. The sun's outermost layer begins about 10,000 miles (16,000 kilometers) above the visible surface and goes outward for millions of miles. This is the only part of the sun that can be seen during an eclipse such as the one Shaun Mankota saw in February 1979. At any other time, the corona can be seen only when special instruments are used on cameras and telescopes to shut out the glare of the sun's rays.

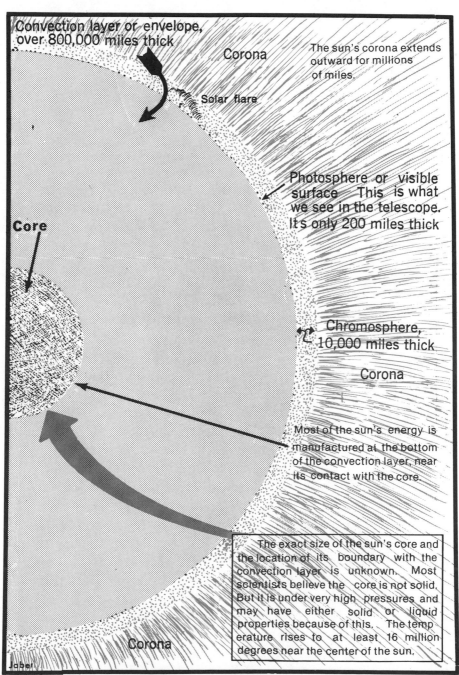

Convection layer or envelope, over 800,000 miles thick

Corona

The sun's corona extends outward for millions of miles.

Solar flare

Photosphere or visible surface This is what we see in the telescope. It's only 200 miles thick

Core

Chromosphere, 10,000 miles thick

Corona

Most of the sun's energy is manufactured at the bottom of the convection layer, near its contact with the core.

The exact size of the sun's core and the location of its boundary with the convection layer is unknown. Most scientists believe the core is not solid. But it is under very high pressures and may have either solid or liquid properties because of this. The temperature rises to at least 16 million degrees near the center of the sun.

Corona

Jaber

THE SUN'S INTERIOR and CORONA

The corona is a brilliant, pearly white, filmy light, about as bright as the full moon. Its beautiful rays are a sensational sight during an eclipse. The corona's rays flash out in a brilliant fan that has wispy spikelike rays near the sun's north and south poles. The corona is thickest at the sun's equator.

The corona rays are made up of gases streaming outward at tremendous speeds and reaching a temperature of more than 2 million degrees Fahrenheit. The rays of gas thin out as they reach the space around the planets. By the time the sun's corona rays reach the earth, they are weak and invisible.

Up to 1930, the corona could be seen only during a total eclipse of the sun. But in that year, the French solar astronomer, Bernard Lyot (lee-óh) invented the coronagraph, an instrument that makes the corona visible at all times.

Chromosphere (kroh-moh-sfeer). The chromosphere is a layer of hot gases just under the corona and above the third zone, or photosphere. It is about 10,000 miles (16,000 kilometers) thick. The gas particles that make up the chromosphere are spaced so far apart and are moving so fast (hundreds of miles per second) that this zone is very hard to see. In addition, the photosphere below it is so brilliant that the chromosphere is almost lost in its glare. Therefore, like the corona, the chromosphere, too, can be viewed only during a total eclipse or by using Dr. Lyot's coronagraph.

The upper part of the chromosphere is astonishing and very beautiful. Jets of hot gases are constantly shooting upward through the chromosphere from the photosphere below. These hot jets are called *spicules*. They surge upward for 10,000 miles or so and spew their gases into the corona above.

51

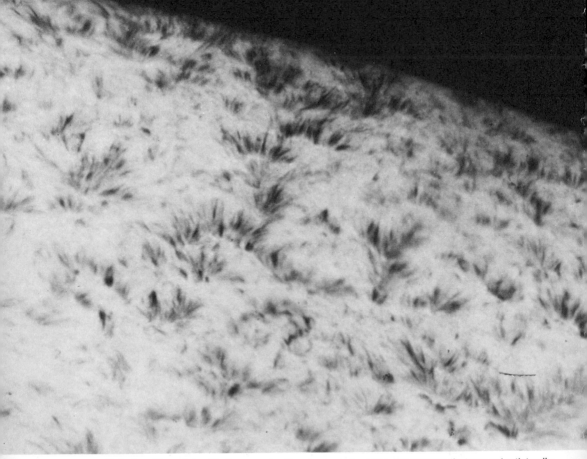

Spicules. These jets of hot gases give the chromosphere the appearance that one scientist calls "flaming forests."

Courtesy Hale Observatories

The chromosphere is the layer where solar flares happen. A *solar flare* is a sudden burst of bright light. It lasts from a few minutes to a few hours. It is made up mainly of hydrogen gas, the lightest and most plentiful gas in the sun.

Solar flares are caused by gigantic magnetic storms, which begin deep inside the sun. *Magnetism*, like radio waves and electricity, is a form of energy. In fact, all these forms of energy, plus others such as X-rays, are all created in the sun and can be found shooting out of the sun into the corona at any time. They all shoot upward at terrific speeds. The magnetic energy has a powerful effect on hydrogen gas. During the storm the gas glows and forms the visible part of the solar flare.

Energy from solar flares often reaches the earth and sometimes cause electrical distribances, such as static on radios and interruptions to television service.

Another feature of the chromosphere is the prominence. A *prominence* is an eruption of a long, ribbonlike mass of hydrogen gas. It is from 10,000 to 30,000 degrees Fahrenheit in temperature and is associated with sunspots, which are described later. A prominence is similar to a flare, but it is slower in forming and lasts longer.

A prominence, 100,000 miles high.

Courtesy Hale Observatories

Photosphere. The photosphere is the part of the sun we see, the part which gives off the brilliant, blinding glare of light. It is a layer of dense gas about 200 miles thick and has a temperature of around 5,000 degrees Fahrenheit at the top, where it merges with the chromosphere. At the bottom, where it is in contact with the convection zone, it has a temperature of about 9,000 degrees.

The massive, boiling convection zone below is what feeds the photosphere its energy and glare. In addition, the gigantic volume of energy that the sun produces in its deeper areas roars up through the photosphere in great columns. Most of this energy is funneled

The photosphere.

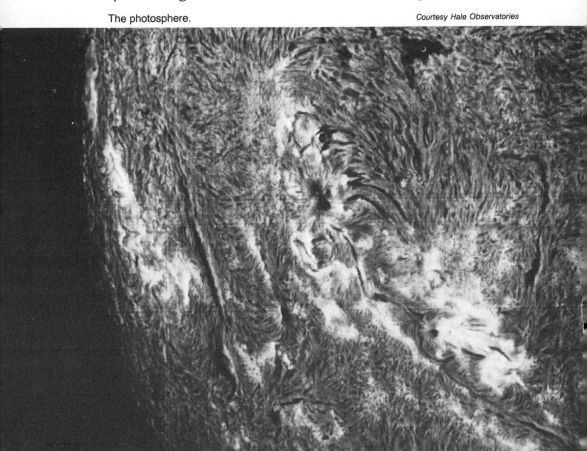

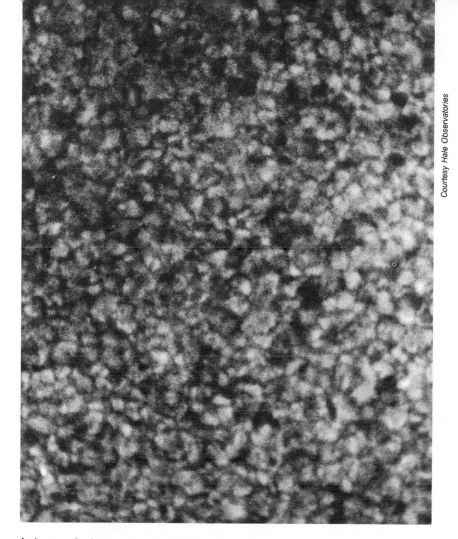

A closeup of solar granules. Each of these "grains" is really the top of a column of hot gas, up to 500 miles across and thousands of miles deep.

out of the sun through the corona, and this is what we feel here on earth as the warming rays of the sun. Almost all the light we get from the sun also comes from this zone.

It is the very top of the photosphere that we see in photographs.

The photosphere appears grainy in a close-up

55

photo, and it is. It is made up of millions of grainlike structures called *granules*. Sometimes the whole surface of the sun looks like a mass of rice grains. But each grain is up to 500 miles wide and is actually the top of a gigantic column of gas. These columns are driven upward by the energy that is being created deep inside the sun. Granulation is a permanent feature of the sun.

Most of the sun's energy output from its interior zones reaches the upper layers through the granules. From the granules, the sun's heat and light shoot upward and outward in all directions.

Although the granular process, or granulation, is a permanent feature of the sun's surface, each granule lasts only a few minutes. Therefore, the sun's surface at the photosphere is in constant motion. This motion consists of energy and gases being driven, mostly upward. But some of the gases cool rapidly, and thus darken and move sideways, and then down into the sun again. These gases go back down into the sun around the edges of the granules. This action accounts for the shape and color of the granules.

Sunspots are cooler areas in the photosphere that show up as dark spots. This is because cooler gases are darker in color than are the surrounding hotter gases. A sunspot is made up of a central region called the *umbra* and a cooler surrounding area called the *penumbra*. Spots range in size from about 900 miles across to nearly 10,000 miles across—nearly as large as the earth. They are temporary in nature, unlike the permanent granules.

Sunspots are very active and have different shapes. Gases flow from the hotter central umbra to the cooler outer penumbra at a rate of about 2 miles per second. The shapes often change, and two spots may even combine to form one.

Sunspots "break out," that is, they appear suddenly, usually in groups of two or more in the same area and on either side of the sun's equator. There is a regular cycle of sunspot activity. It is associated with what astronomers call the *solar cycle*. This is a period of about 11 years during which changes in the sun happen according to a regular pattern.

A large group of sunspots. Note the clear division between the umbra and the surrounding penumbra. And note also the "rice grain" granules around the sunspots. This group of sunspots is as large as our earth.

Courtesy Hale Observatories

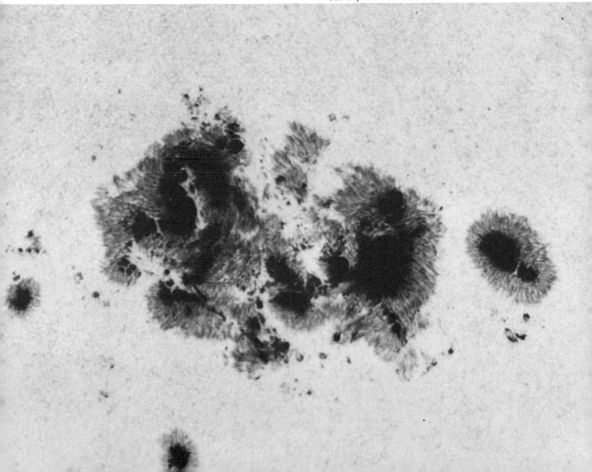

Another view
of sunspots,
closer up.

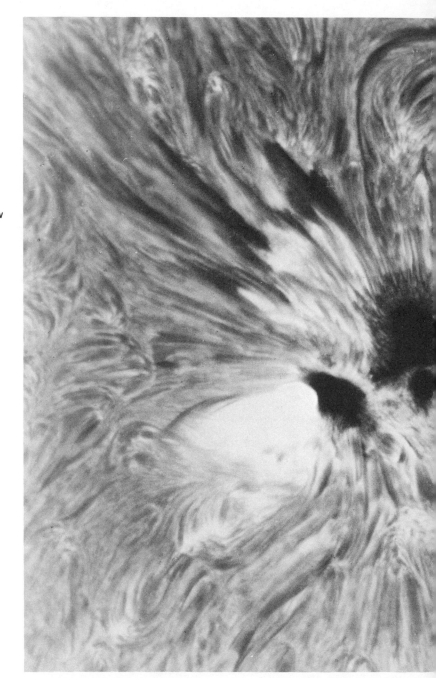

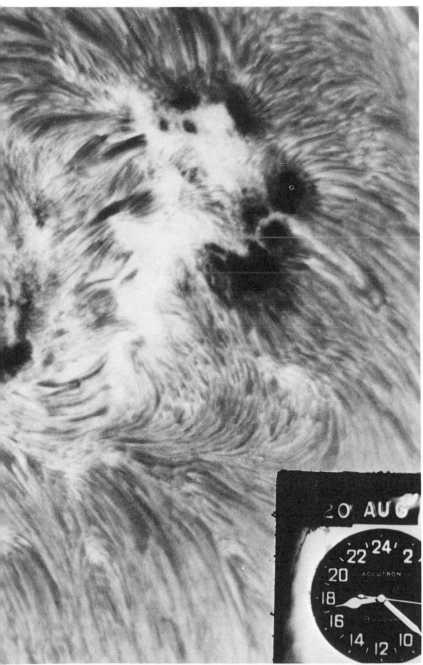

Courtesy Hale Observatories

59

THE SOLAR CYCLE

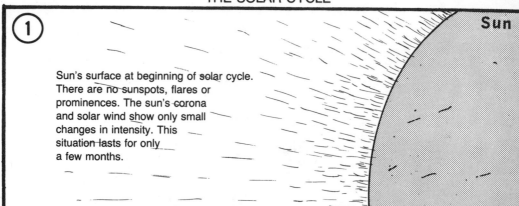

① Sun

Sun's surface at beginning of solar cycle. There are no sunspots, flares or prominences. The sun's corona and solar wind show only small changes in intensity. This situation lasts for only a few months.

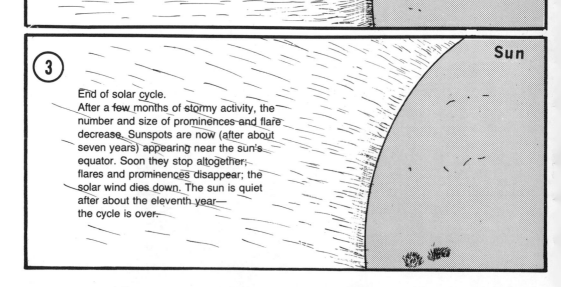

② Sun

Sunspots appear at high latitudes, marking the beginning of the cycle. At first, they last only a few days. After a year or so the sunspots begin to break out of lower latitudes and last longer. Flares begin to appear near the sunspots. These shoot streams of energy and particles high up into the corona. After about 4 and one-half years, the sun reaches the height of its activity, marked by the appearance of prominences, and storms of solar wind.

③ Sun

End of solar cycle. After a few months of stormy activity, the number and size of prominences and flare decrease. Sunspots are now (after about seven years) appearing near the sun's equator. Soon they stop altogether; flares and prominences disappear; the solar wind dies down. The sun is quiet after about the eleventh year— the cycle is over.

The Solar Cycle

All the sun's zones contribute to the solar cycle but it is not yet clear how and why the solar cycle takes place. Each cycle begins with an outbreak of sunspots at about the same time at high altitudes near both poles of the sun. The first spots are followed in a few hours or days by others, each breaking out closer and closer to the equator. Since the sun's surface is rotating on its axis all this time, the sunspots never break out in the same place, because once a spot has broken out, it moves along as the sun rotates.

At the height of the solar cycle, about 5 years after the first spots, there are 100 times more spots breaking out than in the first year or so. Each of the spots lasts from a few days to several weeks. Since the sun is rotating, some spots are carried right across the face of the sun and around the back side.

Before the last spots have died out near the equator, thus ending the old cycle (after about 11 years), the first new spots have already appeared near the poles, opening a new cycle.

But the sunspots are not the only happenings in the solar cycle. There is an increase in other solar activity early in the cycle. Solar flares break out more often, as do prominences. And at the height of the cycle, a great deal of energy, gas, and other particles are brought up through the zones and pass out through the corona—much more energy than at other times. It is during these high periods of solar activity that the sun affects television and radio on the earth. The details of this activity are reserved for the next chapter.

But almost as suddenly as it all began, the sun quiets down again, and the cycle begins all over. Each cycle has a quiet phase and an active phase. During the quiet phase, the sun's surface is free of sunspots for several months at a time. In 1979, the sun entered the height of its 11-year cycle. Solar activity will be increasing until about 1982.

Convection Zone. The convection zone forms the bulk of the sun. It is over 800,000 miles thick and ranges in temperature from about 200,000 degrees at the top to perhaps more than 15 million degrees where it contacts the sun's core.

We can never see or visit this region. Our knowledge of it comes from laboratory experiments and from direct observations of other parts of the sun. This is the zone where most of the sun's energy is created, especially at the point where the zone comes into contact with the core or gradually changes into the core. How this massive energy is created is the subject of the next chapter.

Chapter 6 How the Sun Makes Its Energy

In just one second the sun sends out more energy than human beings have used in all the 6,000 years of recorded history! How does the sun produce this staggering load of energy?

The exact way in which it is done is very complex and cannot be described here in detail, but the process can be outlined in a general way.

The most plentiful matter in the sun is hydrogen, which is the lightest matter known in the whole universe. Because it is light, hydrogen is the first to break apart when put under great heat and pressure. There is no place in the universe with more heat or pressure than inside a star, and the sun is a star. So the hydrogen gas is under billions and billions of tons of pressure per square inch, and toward the center of the sun it has a temperature of more than 16 million degrees Fahrenheit. The pressure comes from the weight of the gases above, so the pressure is greatest at the center.

The gases of the sun are simply the materials and matter we have here on earth but which are so hot that they cannot exist in a solid form. The basic particle of all matter is the atom. For example, iron is made up of iron atoms. An *atom* is the smallest unit of any material which still has the characteristics of that material. An atom of iron is the smallest unit into which iron could be broken and still be called iron. If the atom of iron is broken, what comes out of it is no longer iron but a large amount of energy plus some other material that would be lighter than iron. This could only happen under conditions of great heat and pressure, such as those which occur in the sun.

Now that we know what gases in the sun are and what the conditions there are, we can expect something to happen to the hydrogen, the lightest of the gases.

The pressures are so great and the temperatures so high that no matter in the universe could go through such conditions without changing in some way. And this brings us to what happens to the hydrogen.

Deep inside the sun, at the bottom of the convection zone where the heat and pressures are very high, the hydrogen begins to come apart—it is literally crushed—and converts into a different kind of matter— helium, a slightly heavier gas.

But in the process of changing, some of the hydrogen is lost—it is actually converted into energy. The whole process is called *nuclear fusion*. Nuclear fusion in the sun is the most powerful happening in the universe. It is a process that goes on in all stars until they run out of hydrogen.

Because scientists understood nuclear fusion in the sun, they were able to duplicate the process on earth experimentally, and the result was—the hydrogen bomb. It could destroy an entire country if it were ever used in war. But scientists now think that some day soon they will be able to control nuclear fusion and so release the

THE NUCLEAR FUSION PROCESS

Two hydrogen atoms.

Nuclear fusion is the joining together of the
center parts or nuclei of two light hydrogen atoms
to form the center or nucleus of a heavier atom: helium

Fusion can happen only under terrific heat and pressure
—like that of the sun. The heat forces the atoms
to move at super speeds even though they are under
heavy pressure.

When two hydrogen atoms collide under these conditions,
the shock is so great. . . .

. . . They crush each other and fuse, with a great explosive
force. This action destroys part of
both atoms, converting those parts
to energy. The energy moves upward
and out of the sun in the form of
radiation such as light, X-rays,
radio waves, etc.

What remains after the explosion is a single, slightly
heavier atom called helium. Billions of these fusion
explosions happen every second in the sun, and will
go on happening until all the hydrogen is used up,
which will take billions of years. 65

great energy slowly, to generate electricity and for other purposes.

Inside the sun, the energy created by nuclear fusion moves upward through all the zones and to the outside of the sun, where it becomes part of the corona and then trails off and away from the sun at terrific speeds. We mentioned earlier that this energy consists of radio waves, electricity, light, and even X-rays. All these forms of solar energy are called *wave energy*, because they move in waves as described earlier under radio waves.

But in addition to this solar wave energy, the nuclear fusion process in the sun creates other kinds of energy, called *particle energy*. Particle energy consists of bits and pieces of matter called *particles*. Particles are so small that even a microscope cannot detect some of them. And they, too, move out from the sun, but not quite as fast as wave energy moves.

The particles speed out at the rate of from 200 to 500 miles per second. When they reach outer space, around the sun, the particles are called the *solar wind*. They are called a wind because the tiny particles are moving at such a high speed that they act like a wind.

Like any wind, the solar wind cannot be seen, but its presence is felt all the time. It causes static on radios and interrupts television broadcasts. And the solar wind causes the display of light in the sky known as the *aurora borealis*, or northern lights, and the *aurora australis*, or southern lights.

The National Aeronautics and Space Administration (NASA) has considered using the solar wind as a means of travel. A *solar sail* has been designed that could move along on the solar wind for billions of miles in the space between the planets. A spaceship with a solar sail

The solar sail is a huge canopy made of very light but dense material. The solar wind will push against it just as the earth's winds push against the sails of ships. A satellite or space laboratory would be attached to the solar sail. Of course, because the solar wind's strength decreases as the sail moves further away from the sun, the sail is only good for travel between the planets nearer to the sun—Venus, Earth, and Mars.

could move through space without an engine. But the testing of such a sail is years away.

The solar wind could be harmful to astronauts. Some of the particles are so fast and so small that they go right through most materials, such as space suits or metal. And they are either poisonous or harm the body in other ways, such as by causing cancer.

Radiation poisoning from the solar wind is one of the dangers of traveling in outer space.

The process of nuclear fusion in the sun uses up hydrogen at the rate of 4 million tons every second. Suppose it took you ten minutes to read the last chapter. That is 600 seconds. During those 600 seconds, the sun has used up 2 billion, 400 million tons of matter (2,400,000,000). At that rate, could the sun burn itself out in a few years? Not likely. The sun is too large. It is so large that it has been glowing for many billions of years, and still it has enough hydrogen to last another few billion years.

But what will happen when the sun does finally run out of hydrogen? Most astronomers believe that it will swell up into a giant red star and its surface will swallow up all the nearby planets—Mercury, Venus, Mars, and Earth. These astronomers say it will remain a giant red star for a few million years and then will cool

Crab Nebula. This is what remains of a giant star when it explodes. The explosion of Crab Nebula was seen in 1054 A.D. and caused a lot of excitement. Actually, the explosion had taken place 6,300 years before—it took that long for its light to reach us.

Courtesy Lick Observatory

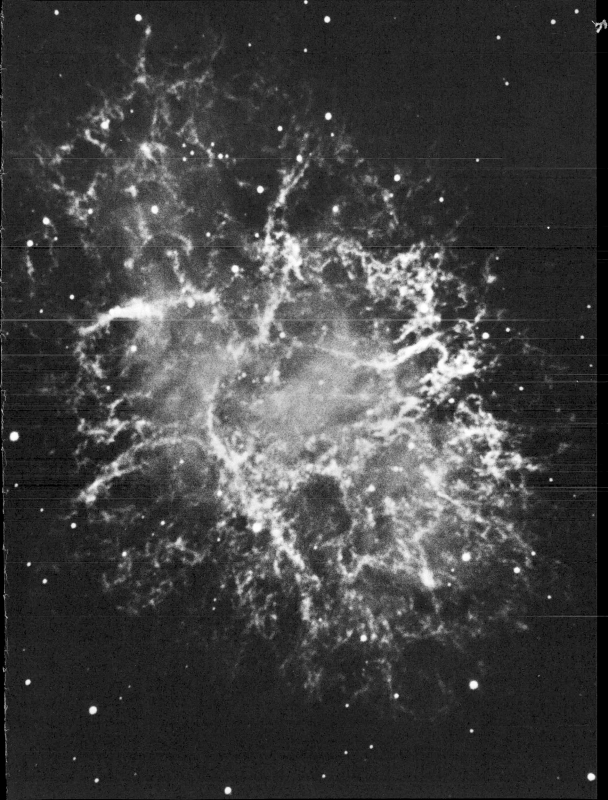

down, shrink in size, and change in color to a white or gray, and then it will be dead. All the fires will go out, and our solar system will move in total blackness, frozen and lifeless for billions of years, or perhaps forever.

Not all astronomers believe the red giant will shrink, cool down, and die. Some say that it will keep on swelling until it explodes in a blinding flash, destroying the entire solar system. It will then be known as a *nova*, and from its ashes a new star will form, perhaps with new worlds circling around it.

It does happen. Scientists have witnessed nova explosions in other stars. The giant Crab Nebula is a cloud of space dust and particles, about 6,300 light years away, but clearly visible through large telescopes. It is the remains of a star whose explosion was witnessed and recorded by observers here on the earth in July of 1054 A.D. Of course, since the light of that explosion had been traveling for 6,300 years before it reached the earth, the explosion actually took place long before there was a civilization on this earth.

Whatever the sun's fate, it has a long life ahead. It is not yet an old star. Perhaps by the time it is old and ready to die, humans will be able to move out of the solar system.

Chapter 7   Life and Energy from the Sun

The sun's radiant energy has lighted and warmed the earth for at least 6 billion years. In fact, most astronomers believe the earth was formed out of the sun in some as yet unexplained way. Perhaps a passing star nearly crashed into it. Some astronomers believe that such a near miss would have caused a great bulge in the sun, and enough material would have spewed out to form the sun's present family of planets and their moons.

But there are other theories, too, ideas still to be proven. One is that the solar system (the sun's family) and the sun itself were created at the same time from the ashes and broken pieces of a giant star that exploded.

Whatever the nature of the beginning, one thing is certain: the sun's heat and other forms of energy heated up the earth's atmosphere, rocks, and water. This gave rise to temperatures that remained steady and dependable for millions of years. Most scientists believe that life began accidentally as a mixture of water and various kinds of chemicals, which were affected by the solar wind and the strong, steady light from the sun. The basic elements of life have been created in laboratories where these ancient conditions were duplicated.

Scientists agree, therefore, that the sun is the source of life. And ever since life has existed on the earth, the sun has kept some parts of the planet warm and suitable for the continued evolution of life. The sun's dependability as a source of heat and light gave an opportunity for plants and animals to develop and spread all around the world.

For millions of years, the sun's energy was used by plants to manufacture cellulose. *Cellulose*, or plant fiber, is a *carbohydrate*, a form of food. Sugar and starch are two other main kinds of carbohydrates.

Without plants, life as we know it would have been impossible. Plants built up the carbohydrates and animals fed on them. One could not do without the other. It was the sun that supported it all by giving warmth and by providing the plants with the energy they used in the manufacture of carbohydrates.

Forests, jungles, swamps, and grasslands began to grow on all the continents about 350 million years ago. The oceans, lakes, and rivers were already filled with living things, such as fish, shellfish, and water plants.

For millions of years, plants and animals by the millions and millions lived and died in the same areas. In some places, especially low, swampy valleys and along tropical shores, the remains of dead plants and animals piled up in thick layers, forming such heavy masses that the land slowly sank under their weight.

Over a few million years, these remains of plants and animals were slowly changed into layers of fossils. *Fossils* are the hard parts of plants and animals, such as shells, bones, leaves, and stems, or they are a record of life, such as footprints or impressions in stone. Fossils are preserved in the rocks by natural processes.

Under conditions of pressure of weight and heat, also caused by great weight, many of the layers of fossils became coal, peat, lignite, petroleum, and natural gas—five kinds of fossil fuels. These are really just stored

Fossil

This fossil, imbedded in a piece of rock, is the preserved remains of a trilobite, a crablike animal that has been extinct for over 200 million years.

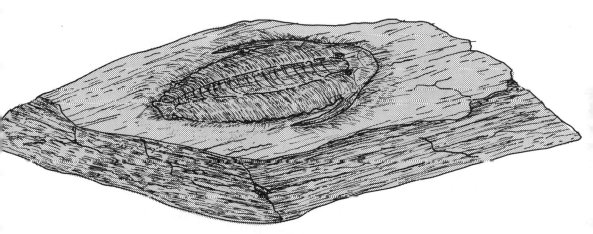

energy—solar energy, or energy the sun beamed down to the earth millions of years ago.

Most of the stored energy that lies buried in the earth's crust has been there for millions of years. It was not used until there were humans with brains and cultures capable of using the sun's stored energy—fossil fuels. Humans began to dig coal and later to drill for petroleum and natural gas. They burned these fuels to heat water, cook food, warm themselves, and run their machines. They also used the fossil fuels to make other forms of energy, such as electricity.

Scientists have known for hundreds of years that the sun's rays can also be used directly as energy. They knew that the sun's light and heat could do work.

For example, thousands of years ago, people would drain water from bays and inlets into low, flat areas where the sun would dry up all the water, leaving valuable salt, which they used to season and preserve food.

One of the earliest uses of solar energy was for heating. Buildings were often constructed in a way that allowed the sun's warming rays to enter during the cool mornings and be blocked from entering the house in the afternoon, when it was hot.

The sun's rays were also used to send messages. In the American West shortly after the Civil War, cavalry troops kept in touch with each other by using a *heliograph*. This was a machine that looked like an old-fashioned camera, mounted on a tripod, or three-legged stand. It had a shutter which fit over a mirror. When the heliograph was turned toward the sun, its rays struck the mirror and could be beamed across deserts and valleys. The beam or reflected rays, could be broken by the shutter so that the beams of light flashed. These flashes were developed as a code, following the Morse code. The Morse code uses dots and dashes, which the heliograph turned into short flashes for dots and long flashes for dashes.

The sun's energy was also used to purify water. This was done by using a glass or mirror to collect the sun's rays together—focus them, which made the sun's energy much more powerful. When a pot of water was set under such focused energy, the water would quickly boil. When water is turned into steam or vapor by boiling, it drops all its dirt and other impurities. Then, when the steam or vapor is cooled, it turns back into a liquid, suitable for drinking. This process is called *distilling*. It is used very often today.

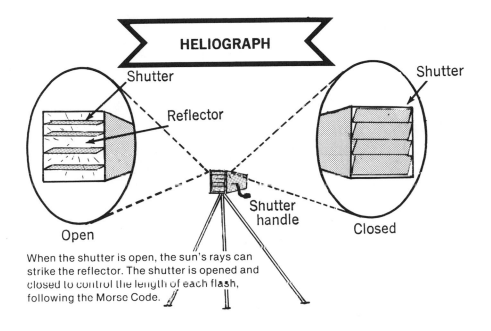

HELIOGRAPH

Shutter

Reflector

Shutter

Open

Closed

Shutter
handle

When the shutter is open, the sun's rays can strike the reflector. The shutter is opened and closed to control the length of each flash, following the Morse Code.

Scientists feel that someday the sun's energy will be used to distill water from the ocean more cheaply than it can be distilled by other means today.

The sun's heat energy is now being used to melt thick metal such as steel. This is done in a *solar furnace*, which concentrates the sun's rays. The furnace works by mirrors that can move automatically to follow the sun's path across the sky. The sun's rays strike the mirrors and are reflected off them and concentrated on a tiny spot in front of them. The spot can get as hot as 6,300 degrees Fahrenheit. A piece of metal there would be burned through in seconds. Most scientists feel that in the near future the solar furnace will be a valuable and inexpensive way to melt, mix, and work with metals.

75

HOW A SOLAR FURNACE WORKS

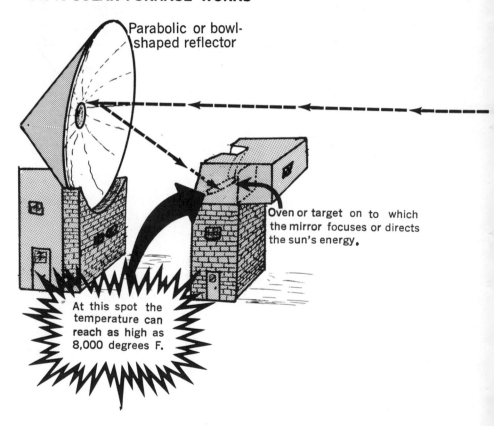

Parabolic or bowl-shaped reflector

Oven or target on to which the mirror focuses or directs the sun's energy.

At this spot the temperature can reach as high as 8,000 degrees F.

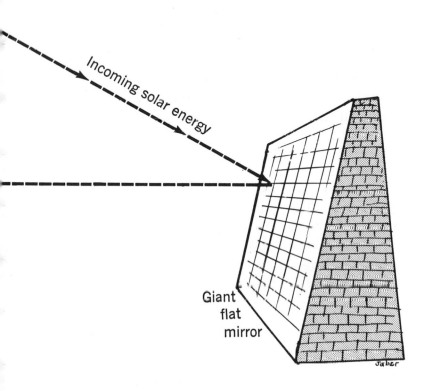

Incoming solar energy

Giant
flat
mirror

Jaber

Solar energy is coming into use today for heating water in homes and swimming pools, and for air conditioning homes. Most solar hot-water heaters for homes use a flat-plate collector. This is a flat box with a black-colored bottom and a glass over the top. Black is a color that absorbs solar heat. Water flows through metal or glass tubes that are spaced out under the box's black bottom. The collector is usually mounted on the roof of the house. Sometimes it can be tilted or rotated to help keep the sun shining directly on its surface.

The main way to use solar energy in industry is to generate electricity with it. There are several ways to do this. But the one scientists are beginning to consider most is the *solar cell*. This is a small device that can convert sunlight into an electric current. But the current is very weak, and so many of the devices are needed and are strung together. The current builds up in proportion to how many of the solar cells are used.

At present the solar cells cost a lot of money to produce. And because each of them produces such a weak current, they are not very efficient—that is, they can use only 10–15 percent of the solar energy that strikes them. The amount of current produced is so small that hundreds of the cells are needed to run something like a radio or a telephone or a computer.

However, spacecraft have long been using solar cells. For them it is the cheapest way to produce electricity in outer space. But on the ground, the cost per cell is still too high. We can still generate electricity by other means cheaper than we can by using solar cells. That means that the solar cells have to be improved.

A Roof Solar Heat Collector Panel

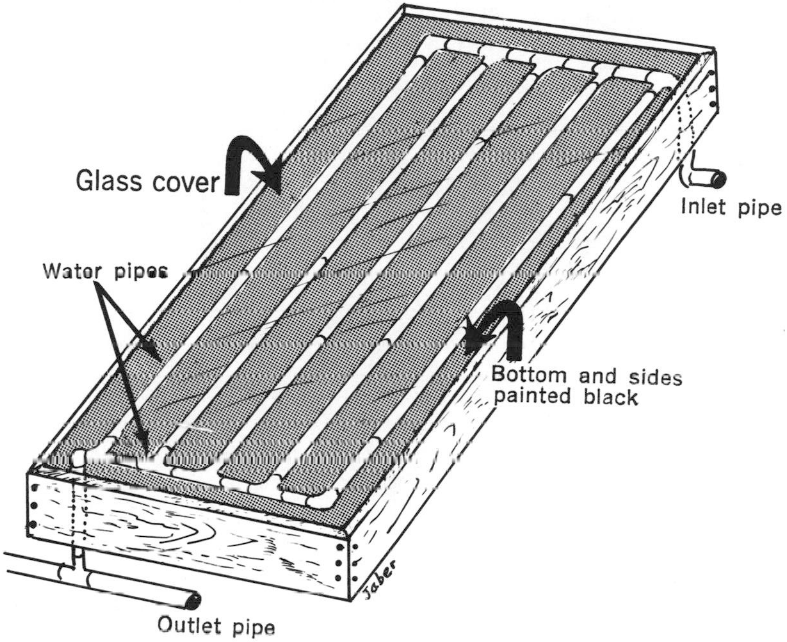

Glass cover

Water pipes

Inlet pipe

Bottom and sides
painted black

Outlet pipe

The sun's heat energy is absorbed by the black sides and bottom of the collector. The glass traps it so that the box gets very hot inside. The trapped heat makes the pipes hot. Water circulating in the pipes is heated and then carried through the house to supply heat and hot water.

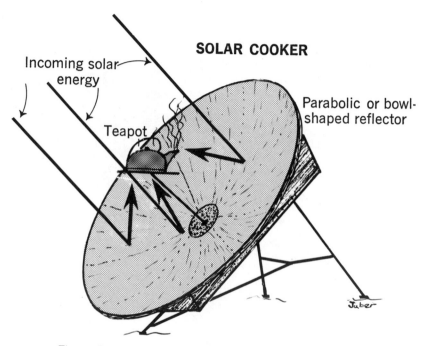

SOLAR COOKER

Incoming solar energy

Teapot

Parabolic or bowl-shaped reflector

The sun's rays strike the reflector's curved surface. This surface helps to focus the rays on to the spot where a pot or teakettle is placed.

But as the price of petroleum continues to go higher, scientists are turning more and more toward the sun as a source of energy to replace the expensive petroleum and natural gas.

They are searching for ways to make the solar cell less expensive to produce. Most scientists are very optimistic about the future of solar energy. It is steady, faithful, and predictable. Scientists say that the sun's energy output has not gone down more than about 3–5 percent in the last billion years.

How amazed the ancients would have been to learn all these things about the sun—Shaun Mankota would be, also. And although the sun worship of the ancients was instinctive, science has shown that the sun, while not a god, is indeed the giver, the basis, of all life. We, too, must surely revere the source of life, our sun.

Courtesy Hale Observatories

A total eclipse of the sun.

 **Glossary**

Atmosphere—the outer gaseous envelope or covering surrounding any heavenly body, including the earth.

Aurora Australis—a display of colored lighting high in the sky in the Southern Hemisphere. It is a complex electrical effect caused by the solar wind as it strikes the earth's atmosphere. *See also* Solar Wind.

Aurora Borealis—a display of colored lighting high in the sky in the Northern Hemisphere. *See also* Aurora Australis.

Carbohydrates—plant food substance, manufactured by plants, using the sun's energy. Sugar, starch and plant fiber or cellulose are the three main carbohydrates. They are the basis of all life on the earth.

Carbon dioxide—a gas, one of the main gases found in the earth's atmosphere, which is a mixture of gases.

Chromosphere—a layer of hot gases just under the sun's corona. It is about 10,000 miles thick and is where solar flares and prominences happen.

Convection Zone—the main body of the sun. It is the whole bulk that lies just under the photosphere. It is 800,000 miles thick, going nearly to the center of the sun. At its bottom, near the sun's center, is the place where most of the sun's energy is produced.

Core—the center of the sun. Some scientists believe it may be a liquid or even a solid body, but no one knows. Its temperature is known to be about 20 million degrees Fahrenheit.

Corona—the sun's outermost layer. It is millions of miles thick because it goes out even beyond the orbits of the inner planets, including the earth. Most of the corona is invisible in ordinary light, but that part near the sun can be seen in a total eclipse or when a coronagraph is used to shut out the sun's glare.

Coronagraph—a machine that makes the corona visible even without an eclipse. It is used to study the sun's corona.

Distilling—the process of boiling water until it turns to steam or vapor, after which it drops all its impurities. The steam is then cooled and it becomes a liquid again—clean water.

Electricity—one of the main forms of wave energy made deep inside the sun. It can also be generated on the earth with special machines called generators or dynamos. Electricity can hurt you.

Energy—the ability to do work—any kind of work. There are many forms of energy. Those made inside the sun include various wave energies such as radio waves, X-rays, light (which is a mixture of several kinds of wave energy) and electricity or electrical energy.

Fossil Fuel—any fuel made from the remains of plants and animals that died long ago. Coal, petroleum and natural gas are fossil fuels.

Galaxy—a large group of stars, usually orbiting or moving around a central area of space. A galaxy may contain billions of stars. Our galaxy is called the Milky Way, and contains about 100 billion stars.

Granules—grain-like features on the photosphere of the sun. Each is up to 500 miles across. Granules are the tops of towering columns of hot gases com-

ing up out of the sun's interior. When photographed in certain kinds of light they look like
rice grains.

Heliograph—a machine to send messages across a distance using reflected sunlight. The machine has
a shutter and looks like a camera. Its shutters
can flash out the Morse code, using short
flashes for the Morse code dots and long flashes
for the Morse code dashes.

Horizon—the farthest point that a person can see.

Hydrogen—the lightest substance in the universe. In the
sun it is a gas, and is used in the nuclear fusion
process to produce helium and energy. *See also*
Nuclear Fusion.

Light Year—the distance light travels in one year at
186,000 miles per second.

Magnetism—another main form of energy. It is similar to
electricity, but unlike electricity, it will not hurt
you.

Milky Way—the name of our own galaxy.

Mirage—seeing something that is not there, but is usually a reflection of something that exists far
away. *See also* Optical Illusion.

Nitrogen—the most plentiful gas found in the earth's atmosphere, which is a mixture of gases. About 75
percent of the air is nitrogen.

Nova—the remains of a star that has exploded. A super-
nova is the remains of a giant star that exploded.
These are usually seen as huge clouds of gas.

Nuclear Fusion—the most powerful natural process in
the universe. It goes on in all stars, and results
in the conversion of hydrogen gas to helium
gas, with the release of gigantic amounts of
energy. It is the way the sun makes its energy.

Optical Illusion—seeing something that is very different from the way it really is. It is not like a mirage, which is seeing something that is not there at all.

Orbit—the path of any heavenly body around any other heavenly body, or around some central point.

Oxygen—one of the important gases in the earth's atmosphere which is a mixture of gases. On the average it makes up 20 percent of the atmosphere, and is necessary for life.

Particles—fast moving bits of substance or matter. They are one of the products of nuclear fusion in the sun.

Penumbra—the outer region of a sunspot. It is cooler than the surrounding photosphere by about 500 degrees, but it is hotter than the umbra which it surrounds.

Pharaoh—the title of ancient Egyptian kings. The word actually means "great house," and originally referred to the king's palace, not the person in it.

Photosphere—the layer of the sun we actually are seeing when we look at the sun in natural light, or at a photograph taken in natural light. It is only about 200 miles thick, and lies between the Chromosphere above and the Convection zone below it.

Prominence—a gigantic storm or eruption on the sun. A fiery plume or arch forms, lasts from several hours to several months and then weakens and disappears. Sometimes the solar gases that make up a prominence fall back along the same path they came up. They can be up to 200,000 miles long, and big enough to swallow several earths.

Radiation—the general name for all the particles that are made and blasted out of the sun in the nuclear fusion process. Radiation can be dangerous to living things.

Radio—the name of the machine used to capture radio wave energy. *See also* transmitter.

Radio Wave—a form of solar energy. Radio waves can also be generated on the earth and are often used to measure distances between the earth and other heavenly bodies.

Saros—a lunar or moon cycle of 18 years and 11 days, or 223 trips of the moon around the world, after which the moon moves in front of the sun causing a total solar eclipse.

Satellite—a natural or artificial body that orbits another body in space. The natural satellites of planets are called moons.

Senses—sight, taste, hearing, smell and touch, the senses by which humans sense their surroundings.

Solar Astronomy—the study of the sun as a heavenly body.

Solar Cell—a small complex device that converts sunlight into electricity. It is used in large groups to generate electricity for lights, machines and other equipment on spacecraft or satellites.

Solar Cycle—a period of about 11 or 12 years in which changes in the sun's activities happen in a regular increasing and then decreasing pattern. The number of sunspots, flares and other features increases for about five or six years and then decreases to the end of the cycle. The solar wind and the amount of energy produced by the sun also goes up and down with the cycle.

Solar Energy—the energy made deep inside the sun and

blown out and away as sunlight, and other wave energy, such as X-rays, radio waves and electricity.

Solar Flare—a sudden burst of light that lasts from a few minutes to a few hours. It is made up mainly of hydrogen gas. It can affect broadcasting communications on the earth.

Solar Furnace—a device that concentrates the sun's energy to a single spot, by means of reflecting mirrors. The spot can get as hot as 6,300 degrees Fahrenheit, which is hot enough to melt and mix metals.

Solar Sail—a sail designed to use the solar wind as a force for pushing a spacecraft forward in the same way as a sailboat is moved forward by our atmosphere's wind.

Solar System—the sun's family of planets, their moons, the comets, and asteroids.

Solar Wind—the mass of tiny speeding particles that result from nuclear fusion in the sun. They are blown out of the sun and spewed into space. They race along at from 200 to 500 miles per second. They can be dangerous to the safety of spacecraft, astronauts and cosmonauts. *See also* Radiation, Particles.

Spicule—hot jets of solar gases that surge upward through the chromosphere from the photosphere. They cause the chromosphere to look like a flaming forest.

Sunspot—cooler areas in the photosphere. They are solar features that appear and disappear in a regular pattern, following the 11-year solar cycle.

Transmitter—a machine used to send out radio waves.

Umbra—the central region of a sunspot. It is made up of gases that are up to about 2,000 degrees cooler than the surrounding photosphere.

Volume—a word used when we mean how much something holds.

Wave energy—the forms of energy that are beamed out or blown out of the sun in wave form. All are produced in the sun by the nuclear fusion process, and all travel at the speed of light. They include electricity, radio waves, X-rays, and sunlight which is a mixture of several kinds of wave energy.